HUMAN RIGHTS OF WAR BABIES

RITURAJ BASUMATARY

Copyright © Rituraj Basumatary
All Rights Reserved.

Contents

CHAPTER I

Introduction

War-babies are referred to here as babies born to Bangali women consequent of their being raped by Pakistani soldiers and other criminals who took advantage of the situation of the War of Liberation (March to December 1971). While they are referred to as the 'unwanted children', the 'enemy children', the 'illegitimate children' and more contemptuously the 'bastards', their birth-mothers are also variously referred to as the 'violated women', the 'women', the 'distressed women', the 'rape victims', the 'victims of military repression', the 'affected women' and the 'unfortunate' women. Many birth-mothers committed suicide in order to avoid social stigma. Many pregnant women went to India and other places either to terminate pregnancies or arrange deliveries. Many babies were born at home. But unfortunately, accurate or fairly reliable statistics are not available for any of these categories of victims. The situation has led us to make guesswork and presumptions about the number and fate of war-babies. Some limited evidences are to be found in government and non-government organisations records and in records of foreign missions and missionary organisations.

An Italian medical survey, for example, put the number of victims at 40,000 and the London-based International Planned Parenthood Federation (IPPF) estimated it at 200,000. Dr. Geoffrey Davis, a social worker dealing with the management of war-babies at the time argued that the number could go higher. How many victims got pregnant and delivered babies is absolutely uncertain. A government estimate put it at 300,000. But the methodology adopted for reaching this figure was not sound. According to Dr. Davis, about 200,000 women became pregnant. But it was only his guess and not a study.

Newspaper reports of the time which included interviews of Justice KM Sobhan, Chairperson, BWRP, Sister Margaret Mary of Missionaries of Charity, Dr. Geoffrey Davis, the IPPF personnel such as Odert von Shoultzreveal that 23,000 abortions were performed at various Dhaka clinics by a team of British, American and Australian doctors with assistance from some Bangali counterparts. In a sense, it makes the most comprehensive information on abortion in early 1972 following the arrival of the foreign doctors in Dhaka who set up several abortion/delivery clinics referred to as Seba Sadan in Dhaka.

Newspaper reports indicate that between 300 and 400 children were born in the premises of 22 Seba Sadans which were established across Bangladesh. The Executive Director of the Canadian UNICEF Committee following his visits to both occupied Bangladesh and independent Bangladesh, where he held discussions with representatives of the League of Red Cross Societies and the UNICEF personnel reported to headquarters in Ottawa that the estimated number of the war-babies was nearly 10,000. While no exact records are available to determine the accuracy of such figures, it is probably safe to assume that the number seems incredibly high. Ten thousand is by far the largest number quoted in any record that made reference to the birth of the war-babies in 1972.

CHAPTER II

Rape during the Bangladesh Liberation War

The Birangonas were the victims to a systematic campaign of genocidal rape organized by the Pakistani Military and their supporting Razakars during the 1971 Bangladesh Liberation War. The term Birangona refers to war heroines and was first introduced by Sheikh Mujib in 1971 in an attempt to prevent them from being outcast by the society. The number of victims is said to be greater than the estimated 200,000 to 400,000 with difficulty in recognizing the real count of victims due to deaths which were attributed to suicide, military torture and migration to India.

These rapes caused thousands of unwanted pregnancies resulting in the birth of war babies, abortions, infanticide, suicide and societal ostracization of the victims. The military of West Pakistan raped Bengali women to strengthen the belief that Pakistanis should be the dominant and powerful population taking away their honor and dignity as a way to emasculate the Bengali men who could not protect their own people. These women were forbidden from performing abortions as a way to "purify" the Bengali race and leave a long-lasting mark on Bengali communities. Besides the West Pakistan military identified perpetrators include Indian soldiers as well as Bengali militiamen with certain recounts of Bihari men targeting Hindu women at the time. However due to the political divide, non-Bengali Muslims such as the migrated Bihari populationas well as other Bengalis were allegedly subjected to sexual violence and physical torture on a large scale in districts such as Jessore, Khulna, Mymensingh and Chittagong. The rapes which were committed against non-Bengalis by the "nationalist" Bengalis are deliberately not mentioned in common liberation literature. The psychological and physical trauma that the war had left behind resulted in disruptions of cultural frameworks, that essentially left these women helpless in society. Following the independence of Bangladesh, the rehabilitation of the Birangonas focused on marrying them off or introducing them to the labor market, although the efforts remained unsuccessful as they were subjugated to loss of sociability and public shaming in their villages if revealed that they were victims.

Consequently to prevent the societal and cultural standards of dignified women from being destroyed, there is minimal recognition of the struggle of the Birangona due to the Islamic revivalism which exists in Bengali national identity politics, a situation which has resulted in the censorship of their stories and the destruction of official documents which describe this war atrocity.

In 2009, almost 40 years after the events of 1971, a report which was published by the War Crimes Fact Finding Committee of Bangladesh accused 1,597 people of committing war crimes including rape. Since 2010, the International Crimes Tribunal (ICT) has indicted, tried and sentenced several people to life imprisonment or death for their actions during the conflict. The stories of the rape victims have been told in movies and literature and they have also been depicted in art.

CHAPTER III

Government's initiatives in tackling the problem

The first and most important initiative that the government of Bangladesh took was the creation of a body called Bangladesh Women's Rehabilitation Board (BWRB) on 18 February 1972. Partnering with the Directorate of Training, Research, Evaluation and Communication (TREC) of the Bangladesh Family Planning Association, the Central Organisation for Women's Rehabilitation and the Directorate of Social Welfare of the Ministry of Social Welfare and Labour, the Board had two broad goals - (i) to organize clinical services wherever possible in Bangladesh within the limited time span of three to four months to provide medical treatment to the rape victims & (ii) to plan, organize and establish facilities and institutions specially vocational training centres and to effectively rehabilitate thousands of destitute women in need of immediate help. Destitute women were not necessarily 'violated women' but were considered to be 'war-affected' in that they had lost either their husbands or the bread earners of the family (such as father) killed by the Pakistan Army or had lost their property during the war.

Through its Rehabilitation Programme for the Violated Women, the Government sought innovative ways to enhance the self-esteem of the victims and their status in the nation as noble contributors be regarded with pride. Honouring the unsung heroines, the government had declared that they deserved national recognition for their valiant role in the War of Liberation. In an attempt to find and promote a positive voice around these victims, the government after several rounds of consultation with interest groups came forward to honour them with the title of Birangana (heroines) not as a sign of disgrace and humiliation but as a symbol of honour and courage. By honouring them as such, it was believed that they would be seen as the symbol and embodiment of everything that is descent, courageous and noble. It was also believed that such recognition of sacrifice would open the doors for the Biranganas who would then be accepted by the society as both triumphant and tragic. Simultaneously, the government continued to seek advice from all quarters to formulate its policy on the abandoned war-babies.

CHAPTER IV

Inter-country adoption of the war-babies

Following a personal request of Bangabandhu Sheikh Mujibur Rahman, the US Branch of the Geneva-based International Social Service (ISS) was the first international non-profit organisation to come forward to advise the government concerning the war-babies. Two local voluntary agencies, the Dhaka-based Bangladesh Central Organisation for Women Rehabilitation and the Family Planning Association had worked with the ISS throughout the consultation and implementation phases.

Canada was one of the first countries in the world which had expressed an interest to adopt the war-babies of Bangladesh. Through personal efforts of Mother Teresa and her colleagues at Missionaries of Charity and the government of Bangladesh's Ministry of Labour and Social Welfare, two Canadian organisations got involved in adoptions. They were the Montreal-based Families for Children, a non-profit adoption agency for inter-country adoption and the Toronto-based Kuan-Yin Foundation (pursuing relief of distressed children in the world), a non-profit adoption agency initiated by a group of enthusiastic Canadians. There were other countries such as the US, the UK, France, Belgium, the Netherlands, Sweden and Australia and to name a few. In addition, there were many organisations such as the US-based Holt Adoption Program, Inc and Terre des Hommes.

In facilitating adoption of war-babies by foreign nationals, the government promulgated a Presidential Order entitled The Bangladesh Abandoned Children (Special Provisions) Order 1972. When the first contingent of 15 war-babies from Bangladesh arrived in Canada on 19 July 1972, they received comprehensive media coverage for days. The key media message was that interracial adoption programmes were a positive initiative and that Canadians of diverse background should endorse such an initiative.

CHAPTER V

Discrimination

Children with a parent who was part of an occupying force or whose parent(s) collaborated with enemy forces are innocent of any war crimes committed by parents. Yet these children have often been condemned by descent from the enemy and discriminated against in their society. They also suffer from association with a parent whose war crimes are prosecuted in the post-war years. As such children grew to adolescence and adulthood, many harbored feelings of guilt and shame.

An example are the children born during and after World War II whose fathers were military personnel in regions occupied by Nazi Germany. These children claim they lived with their identity in an inner exile until the 1980s, when some of them officially acknowledged their status. In 1987, Bente Blehr refused anonymity, an interview with her was published in Born Guilty, a collection of 12 interviews with persons whose parent(s) had been associated with German forces in occupied Norway. The first autobiography by the child of a German occupying soldier and Norwegian mother was The Boy from Gimle (1993) by Eystein Eggen. He dedicated his book to all such children. It was published in Norway.

During and in the aftermath of war, women who have voluntary relationships with military personnel of an occupying force have historically been censured by their own society. Women who became pregnant from such unions would often take measures to conceal the father's status.

They commonly chose among the following-

- Arrange a marriage with a local man, who would take responsibility for the child.
- Claim the father was unknown, dead or had left and bring up the child as a single mother.
- Acknowledge the relationship, bring up the child as a single mother.
- Acknowledge the relationship, accept welfare from the occupying force.
- Place the child in an orphanage or give the child up for adoption.
- Emigrate to the occupying country and claim that identity.
- Have an abortion.

After the war, it was common for both mother and child to suffer repercussions from the local population. Such repercussions were widespread throughout Europe. While some women and children suffered torture and deportation, most acts against them fell into one or several of the following categories-

- Name calling- German whore and German kid were common labels.
- Isolation or harassment from the local community and at schools.
- Loss of work.
- Shaving the heads of the mothers (frequently done in the immediate aftermath of the war) in order to publicly identify and shame them.
- Temporary placement in confinement or internment camps.

While repercussions were most widespread immediately after the war, sentiments against the women and their children lingered into the 1950s, 60s and beyond.

CHAPTER VI

War Babies and their Human Rights

"Children born of rape in the context of armed conflict and their mothers are stigmatized, isolated and deprived of resources. They face discrimination in many ways and on many fronts as well as marginalization by their own communities" the UN Committee on the Elimination of Discrimination against Women (CEDAW) and the Child Rights Committee (CRC) said.

The Committees noted these children often do not have their births registered and this lack of official documentation in turn often affects their right to a nationality.

"These obstacles can adversely affect a child's human rights continuing into adulthood as they can encounter huge problems integrating into society" they added.

The two committees called on States parties to comply with their obligations under both the Convention on the Elimination of All Forms of Discrimination against Women and the Convention on the Rights of the Child.

Given the risk of children being rendered stateless, the Committees urged Governments to ensure that children born of rape are registered with a nationality. "In addition, abandoned children should have access to care services" the Committees stressed.

The Committees also highlighted the high levels of violence to which girls are often subjected in conflict situations. "States parties should make all efforts to rescue girls who have been abducted, ensure their integration into society and provide them and their families with access to psychosocial and other rehabilitation services" they said.

CEDAW and the CRC called for accountability for all forms of gender-based violence against women and children including sexual violence and exploitation, sexual slavery, domestic servitude, child and forced marriage as well as the recruitment and use of children during insurgencies and in other slavery-like practices.

They also emphasized the importance of upholding the rights of women and children as central pillars for building and sustaining peace in societies.

CEDAW and CRC are collaborating with the Office of the Special Representative of the UN Secretary-General on Sexual Violence in Conflict to support the implementation of UN Security Council resolutions on women, peace and security/sexual violence in conflict. The joint statement now available online is to inform the forthcoming Secretary-General's special report on this matter.

CHAPTER VII

Conclusion

International participation in the re-habilitation of war-babies had a debatable aspect. The adopting agencies of the West showed more interest in the rehabilitation of war-babies not in their birth-mothers. The war babies were mostly from Muslim women and they were destined to be raised as Christians in the adopting countries, an aspect which made public opinion in Bangladesh quite hostile to inter-country adoption initiative. The war-baby question came to a close by 1974 when the babies were either transported by then to foreign lands as adopted ones or begun to be raised at home as normal domiciles of Bangladesh.